This book belongs to:

_____

It was given to me by:

_____

On:

_____

Bible
Miracles
for Bedtime

JANE LANDRETH
ILLUSTRATED BY JONI WALKER

BARBOUR
PUBLISHING

ISBN 978-1-60260-692-0

Cover and interior illustrations: Joni Walker

Published by Barbour Publishing, Inc., P.O. Box 719, Uhrichsville, Ohio 44683, www.barbourbooks.com

Our mission is to publish and distribute inspirational products offering exceptional value and biblical encouragement to the masses.

Member of the
Evangelical Christian
Publishers Association

Printed in China.
Leo Paper, China; Print Code: D10002132; February 2010

With love to my precious grandsons,
Lane and Cody,
who bring joy and fulfillment
to our lives.

"Everybody living
in Jerusalem knows
they have done an
outstanding miracle,
and we cannot deny it."
Acts 4:16 NIV

Table of Contents

Days of Creation

God saw everything he had made.
And it was very good.
There was evening,
and there was morning.
It was day six.
GENESIS 1:31 NIrV

Have you ever wondered what it was like before God created the world? Close your eyes. It was even darker than that. Then God began His miracle.

God knew someday there would be people. They would need light to work and play. They would need darkness to rest. So God made light to cut through the darkness. Day and night were made on the first day.

God wanted a roof over the earth. On day two, He made the blue sky and puffy white clouds.

There was water everywhere. When God told the water to become rivers, lakes, and seas, dry land appeared. Now plants and trees could grow. This was the third day.

On day four, God made the sun to warm the earth. And He made the moon and stars to shine at night.

Then God made fish to swim in the waters and birds to fly in the sky. This was the fifth day.

On the sixth day, God made all kinds of animals to live on the land.

When God looked at all He had made, He said, "It is very good."

Dear God, You must have had
fun creating the world. I thank
You for making it so beautiful.
Help me take good care of it.
Amen.

Man Made Out of Dust

Then the LORD God took dust
from the ground and formed a man
from it. He breathed the breath of
life into the man's nose, and the man
became a living person.

GENESIS 2:7 NCV

What do you think was God's best creation? If you said people, you're right! God made people special.

God looked at His beautiful world and said, "Now I am ready to make My best creation of all." He picked up some dust from the ground and very carefully formed a man.

God gave the man two eyes to see everything around him. God gave the man a mouth to eat the good food in the garden. God gave the man fingers to feel the furry animals. God gave the man a nose to smell the flowers. God gave the man two feet to walk around the beautiful earth. God gave the man ears so he could hear God talking to him. God called the man "Adam."

Then God gave Adam a job. "Take care of the world," God said.

But there was one more special creation to come. Adam needed a helper. So while Adam was sleeping, God made a woman to be Adam's wife. Adam called the woman "Eve."

Adam and Eve lived in the garden. God gave them everything they needed.

Thank You, God, for making
Your best creation—people—
to live in Your beautiful world.
Thank You for making me a
special creation, too. You are
so great, God. Amen.

The Floating Zoo

> Water flooded the earth for forty days,
> and as it rose it lifted the boat
> off the ground.
>
> GENESIS 7:17 NCV

Have you every wondered what it would be like to take care of the animals at the zoo? Noah found out when he obeyed God.

Noah was God's special friend. One day, God told Noah, "Rain is coming. It's going to rain and rain. Water will cover the whole world. Make a big boat. You and your family will be safe in the boat."

Zzzz went the saws. *Bang, bang* went the hammers.

Soon the boat was finished. God told Noah to take two of every animal into the boat. Two lions padded into the boat. Two rabbits hopped in. Two kangaroos jumped up the ramp. Two snakes crawled in. Two birds flew in. Two of every kind of animal went into the boat.

Then Noah and his family got into the boat. And God shut the door.

It began to rain. It rained and rained and rained. The water outside got deeper and deeper. The big boat floated on the water. And God kept everyone inside the boat safe.

Dear God, You know how to keep
me safe. I thank You for being
with me and taking care of me.
Help me always to trust You.
Amen.

Tower of Babel

[God said,] "Come. Let us go down and mix up their language. Then they will not understand each other."

GENESIS 11:7 NIrV

Have you ever heard someone speak in a different language? Could you understand that person? God created those other languages when people started doing something wrong.

Long ago, everyone on earth spoke the same language. They could all understand each other.

One day someone said, "Let's make some bricks so we can make a tower."

"Yes," said another. "Let's make it tall to reach heaven."

"Then people will see how great we are," someone else said.

The people baked the bricks. *Scrape! Clink!*

Scrape! Clink! They used those bricks to build the tower.

God was watching the people. "These people are trying to be greater than Me," He said. "Let's mix up their language."

God moved among the people, giving them different words. When the people tried to talk to each other, they were confused. They couldn't understand each other. So they stopped building the tower. Many of them moved to different parts of the world.

The city was called Babel, which means "confused." It was there that God mixed up the language of the people.

Dear God, I thank You for
giving me words to talk to my
parents and friends. Help me
to use my words to tell others
about You. Amen.

A Baby for Sarah

Now the LORD was gracious to Sarah as he had said, and the LORD did for Sarah what he had promised.

GENESIS 21:1 NIV

Does your grandma have a baby? Probably not. Most grandmas are too old to have babies. But God promised a very old woman in the Bible that she would have a son.

Her name was Sarah. Sarah was sad. She had always wanted children but she never could.

One day, God spoke to Abraham, Sarah's husband. "Abraham," God said, "I will give you a son."

"But God," Abraham said, "I'm too old to have a son. I'm a hundred years old. And Sarah is ninety!"

"Nothing is impossible with Me," God said.

"A year from now, Sarah will have a son. You will call his name Isaac."

When Sarah heard what God had said, she laughed. *I'm too old*, she thought to herself.

But God did not forget His promise. A year later, just as He said, Abraham and Sarah had a baby boy. Abraham named the baby Isaac, just as God had told him to. And Sarah was happy because God had kept His promise.

Dear God, I thank You
for older people who love me.
May I always show them
love and respect. Amen.

Where Is the Offering?

Abraham answered, "God will give us the lamb for the sacrifice, my son."

GENESIS 22:8 NCV

Have you ever been asked to give up something you loved? Abraham was asked to give up something very special to show his love for God.

God said to Abraham, "Take your son, Isaac, to a place I will show you. Give your son as an offering to Me."

Abraham loved Isaac, but he loved God, too. So he didn't argue with God. He took Isaac to a mountain God showed him.

The father and son started climbing the mountain. They carried wood and fire for a sacrifice.

On the way to the mountaintop, Isaac said,

"Father, we have the wood and fire, but where is the offering?"

Abraham answered, "God will give us one."

Isaac helped Abraham build an altar. Then Abraham laid his son on the altar as an offering, just as God had asked. But suddenly, God's angel called out from heaven. "Abraham! Do not hurt your son."

Abraham looked up and saw a ram in the bushes. He put the ram on the altar instead of Isaac. And Abraham and Isaac worshipped God.

Dear God, please give me
courage when I have something
hard to do. I thank You for
sending Your Son, Jesus, as an
offering for my sins. Amen.

The Burning Bush

There the angel of the LORD appeared to him in flames of fire coming out of a bush. Moses saw that the bush was on fire, but it was not burning up.

EXODUS 3:2 NCV

Are you afraid when you see fire? Moses was once afraid when he saw a burning bush.

One day while Moses was taking care of his sheep, he saw a bush on fire. But he also noticed the bush was not burning up. So he walked closer to the strange sight.

"Moses! Moses!" he heard a voice say.

"Here I am," Moses answered.

The voice said, "Don't come any closer. Take off your shoes. You are on holy ground. I am God."

Moses covered his face because he was afraid.

God said, "I know the troubles My people have suffered in Egypt. They are slaves there. I have heard their cries, and I want to help them. I want you to help Me bring them to a new land."

Moses didn't think he could do that job.

"I will be with you," God said. "I will tell you what to say and do."

Finally, Moses trusted and believed in God. He said, "I will obey You, God."

Dear God, help me remember
that You will keep me safe
when I don't understand what is
happening. I will trust in You
when I am afraid. Amen.

A Stick Became a Snake

The Lord said, "Throw it [a stick] on the ground." So Moses threw it on the ground. It turned into a snake. He ran away from it.

EXODUS 4:3 NIrV

Has your mom ever asked you to do something you didn't think you could do? Moses felt that way when God asked him to lead His people. But God gave Moses a miracle to prove His power.

"I am sending you to bring My people out of Egypt," God told Moses. The people had been slaves to the Pharaoh, the ruler of Egypt.

"What if Pharaoh won't listen to me?" asked Moses.

"What do you have in your hand, Moses?" God asked.

"A stick," answered Moses.

"Throw down the stick," God said.

When Moses threw the stick down, it became a snake.

"Now pick it up," said God.

When Moses picked it up, it became a stick again.

"Show this to Pharaoh," said God. "Then he will believe I sent you."

"But I'm not a good speaker," said Moses. "I don't think I can talk to Pharaoh."

"Then I will send your brother Aaron with you," God told Moses. "He can speak for you."

Moses was glad Aaron was going with him. He knew God would help them show Pharaoh the miracle.

Dear God, sometimes I'm afraid
I can't do what Mom or Dad
asks me to do. Give me courage
and help me to do what is right.
Amen.

Frogs
Everywhere

And Aaron stretched out his hand over the waters of Egypt; and the frogs came up, and covered the land.
EXODUS 8:6 KJV

HOW would you like to sleep with frogs? Does that sound funny? God used frogs and other miracles to show His power to Pharaoh.

Moses and Aaron went to see Pharaoh. "God wants you to let His people go with us," they said. "If you don't let them go, God will make bad things happen here."

"No!" said Pharaoh. So God turned the water of Egypt into blood.

Next God sent frogs. There were so many that people stepped on frogs. They sat on frogs. Frogs were in people's beds. Pharaoh still said, "No!"

Next God sent lice. The tiny bugs got on animals and in people's hair. But Pharaoh said, "No!"

Next the air was filled with flies. But Pharaoh still said, "No!"

Then animals became sick and died. People got sores all over their bodies. A big hailstorm came. Grasshoppers covered the land. God sent darkness on the land. Pharaoh kept saying, "No—God's people cannot go!"

Finally, God sent death to the first son in each family. When Pharaoh's son died, he let the people go free. But God's people had been kept safe.

Dear God, I know that You can
keep me safe when bad things
are happening around me.
You are a powerful God, and
I love You. Amen.

Fire and Clouds

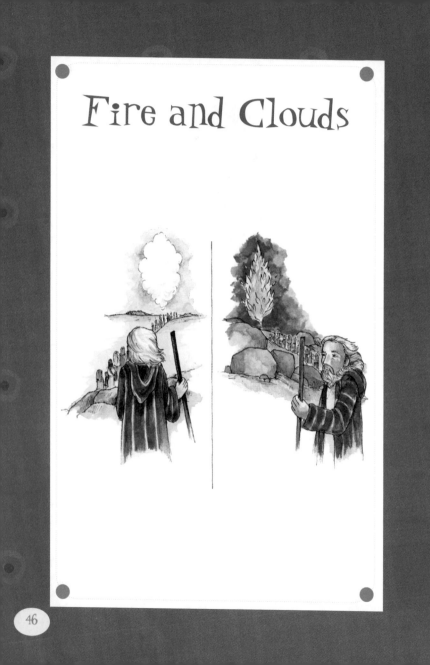

During the day [God] went ahead of
them in a pillar of cloud, and during
the night he was in a pillar of
fire to give them light.

EXODUS 13:21 NCV

Do you like to go on trips? Have you ever
traveled when it was dark? God's people needed
a miracle so they could safely travel day and
night.

God was taking His people on a long, long
trip to a new home. The people were excited.
The women cooked food to take. They filled
water bags. They made big bundles of clothing.
The men got the sheep, goats, cows, and donkeys ready to go.

Soon they started on the long, long trip.
Step, step, step! The people walked down the road.

Clippety-clip, clippety-clop! The animals walked down the road.

"God will take care of us," Moses told the people. "God will lead the way. He will keep us safe."

And God did that in a special way. During the day, God put a big white cloud in the sky. The people followed the cloud. During the night, God put fire in the sky. The fire showed the people God was with them.

The people were glad God was taking care of them on their long, long trip.

Dear God, I like to take trips with my family. I thank You for keeping us safe when we travel. I'm glad You are always with us. Amen.

A Very Big Wind

Then Moses reached his hand out over the Red Sea. All that night the Lord pushed the sea back with a strong east wind. He turned the sea into dry land. The waters were parted.

EXODUS 14:21 NIrV

Do you like to feel the strong wind? God used a strong wind to show a miracle of His power.

Step, step, step went the people. *Clippety-clop* went the animals. Moses was leading them all to a new home.

When the people came to a big sea, they were afraid. There was no way to get across the water. There were no boats to ride in. There were no bridges to walk across.

Moses told the people, "Don't be afraid.

God will help us."

God told Moses to hold his hand over the water.

Whoo-whoo! God sent a big wind to blow. *Whoo-whoo!* The wind blew water to one side. *Whoo-whoo!* The wind blew water to the other side. Right in the middle of the water was a dry path for the people and animals to walk on. They walked to the other side without even getting their feet wet!

Then the wind stopped blowing. All the water splashed together and covered the dry path. The people thanked God for sending the miracle to keep them safe.

Thank You, God, for showing
me Your power in the wind.
Sometimes I am afraid when the
wind blows strong. I know You
can keep me safe. Amen.

Bitter Water
Made Good

So Moses cried out to the LORD, and the LORD showed him a tree. When Moses threw the tree into the water, the water became good to drink.

EXODUS 15:25 NCV

Have you ever been hot and thirsty? Where did you find water? God performed a miracle when Moses and the people were thirsty and could not find water.

Step, step, step! God's people were on a long trip. They walked through the hot, dry desert. There was not much water to drink, but there was a lot of hot sand. God's people tramped across the hot sand. *Step, step, step!*

For three days, God's people traveled in the hot, dry desert. All their water was gone. They couldn't find any more. "We're thirsty!" they cried.

Then someone shouted, "Water! Water!"

The people saw cool water. They ran to the water and took big drinks. *Yuck!* The water tasted bad! It was bitter.

"We can't drink this water," the people complained. "Where will we get good water?"

Moses asked God what to do. God showed Moses a special tree to throw into the water. When Moses threw the tree into the water, the water turned sweet. The people drank the good miracle water.

Thank You, God, for giving
me cool, sweet water to drink.
Help me to remember to pray
whenever I have a problem. You
will always help me. Amen.

Quail and Manna

"I have heard the grumblings of the people of Israel. So tell them, 'At twilight you will eat meat, and every morning you will eat all the bread you want. Then you will know I am the LORD your God.'"

EXODUS 16:12 NCV

Have you ever been really hungry? What would you do if there were no stores where you could buy food? God's people were on a long trip when they ran out of food. So God provided miracle food for them.

God's people were moving to a new home. They had brought food with them but now the food was almost gone. There were no stores where they could buy more food.

The people began to grumble. "We're hungry," they said. "What shall we do?"

Their leader, Moses, talked to God. That night God sent many birds called quail to the people's camp. Now the people had plenty of meat to eat. They were happy.

But God gave them even more. The next morning, the ground was covered with little white flakes. "What is it?" the people asked.

"This is the bread that God sent," said Moses.

The people picked up the bread and tasted it. It was good! The bread was called manna.

God cared for His people.

Thank You, God, for giving
me good food to eat. You love
me and care for me in so many
ways. I thank You that You are
always good to me. Amen.

Hands Held
Up Wins

It turned out that whenever
Moses raised his hands,
Israel was winning,
but whenever he lowered his hands,
Amalek was winning.

EXODUS 17:11 MSG

What do you do when someone wants to fight you? Do you remember to pray for God's help? God helped Moses to win a battle in a strange way.

God's people had a problem. Enemy soldiers attacked the Israelites' camp. The enemy soldiers started to fight God's people.

Moses called his helper, Joshua. He said, "Take some men and fight the enemy!"

Then Moses took two men and climbed a hill. They watched the battle and prayed. When

Moses lifted his hands, God's people began winning the battle.

Soon Moses' hands got tired. They got lower and lower. When he put his hands down, the enemy began to win.

Moses needed help. The two men with Moses found a rock. Moses sat on the rock. The two men stood on each side of Moses and held up Moses's hands. God's people began winning again.

At sunset, the battle was over. God's people had won the battle through a miracle of God.

Dear God, I need Your help
when someone wants to fight me.
I thank You for being near
and showing me the right
thing to do. Amen.

Thunder and Lightning

On the morning of the third day,
there was thunder and
lightning with a thick cloud
on the mountain.
EXODUS 19:16 NCV

Are you afraid when you hear thunder and see lightning? God's people were excited when they heard the thunder and saw the lightning—because God had something special to tell them.

God's people were camped around Mount Sinai. One day, God spoke to Moses, their leader. "Tell the people to get ready. Three days from now, I will come down on Mount Sinai and talk with them."

Moses told the people to get ready. They washed their clothes and cleaned their tents.

Everyone was busy getting ready for God to come talk to them.

Finally, the day came to hear God. A thick cloud hung over Mount Sinai. *Boom! Boom!* Thunder roared. *Zigzag!* Lightning flashed.

Moses led the people close, but not too close! No one was to touch the mountain. No one talked. All was quiet.

Then the people heard God speak. God gave them the Ten Commandments and told them to obey. The commandments were special. They told the people how to live and be happy.

Thank You, God, for the Bible
that tells me how to live
and be happy. I know Your
rules are good. Help me to read
and obey them. Amen.

Then the LORD made the donkey talk,
and she said to Balaam,
"What have I done to make you
hit me three times?"
NUMBERS 22:28 NCV

Do you ever talk to a pet? Have you ever had a pet talk to you? Balaam's donkey talked to him.

A bad king sent his men to get Balaam. He wanted Balaam to hurt God's people with a curse. Balaam saddled his donkey and went to see the bad king.

God was angry with Balaam. He sent an angel to stand in Balaam's way.

When the donkey saw the angel, she left the road. Balaam hit the donkey. They got back on the road.

Then the donkey saw the angel standing between two walls. She moved toward one wall. Balaam's foot was crushed. He hit the donkey again.

Later, when the donkey saw the angel on a pathway, she lay down. Balaam was very angry. He hit the donkey again.

Then God opened the donkey's mouth. "What have I done to make you hit me three times?" she said.

Balaam answered, "You have made me look foolish."

Then God let Balaam see the angel. The angel told Balaam what God wanted him to do.

Dear God, I thank You for pets.
Help me always to be kind
and loving to animals. I know
You want me be kind to all
people, too. Amen.

The Walls
Fall Down

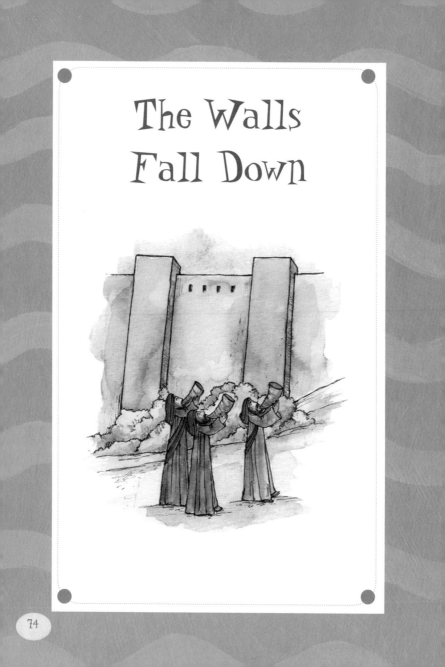

When the priests blew the trumpets,
the people shouted.
At the sound of the trumpets
and the people's shout,
the walls fell.

JOSHUA 6:20 NCV

Do you like to make tall buildings with blocks? Do you ever hit the blocks to make them fall down? God told Joshua to do some strange things to make the walls of Jericho fall. And he didn't even have to touch them.

"I will give you the city of Jericho," God said. "But you must do what I say, Joshua."

"I will obey," said Joshua.

God told Joshua to have the people march around the city one time a day for six days. So for one, two, three, four, five, six days, they marched around the city. All was silent but for the people's footsteps.

On the seventh day, God told Joshua to have the people march around the city seven times. Then the priests were to blow their horns. So the people marched. One, two, three, four, five, six, seven times around Jericho.

The priests blew their horns. Joshua yelled, "Shout!"

The people shouted. *Crash, bang, boom, crumble!* The walls came tumbling down—and no one even touched them. What a miracle!

Dear God, sometimes You ask me
to do things I don't understand.
Help me to obey You because
You always know what is
best for me. Amen.

The Day the Sun Stood Still

So the sun stood still. The moon stopped. They didn't move again until the nation won the battle over its enemies.

JOSHUA 10:13 NIrV

Have you ever been having so much fun that you wished the day were longer? Joshua asked for a longer day to fight an enemy. And God answered with a miracle.

A message was sent to Joshua. It said, "Come, help us! There are five kings and their armies gathering to fight us."

Could Joshua's small army fight five kings and their armies? God told Joshua, "Do not be afraid of them. I will help."

Tramp, tramp! Joshua marched his army into the enemy camp. The enemy soldiers were so surprised that they ran down the road. God dropped large hailstones from the sky on them. Many of the kings' soldiers were killed.

Joshua's army followed the enemy soldiers into the mountains. They needed to find them, or they would come back to fight again. But it was getting dark!

God put an idea into Joshua's mind. Joshua stood up before his army and said, "Sun, stand still!" The sun stood still and did not go down until Joshua's army won the fight! What a great miracle!

Dear God, sometimes You
surprise me with a miracle
when I must do something hard.
I thank You for always being
near when I need help. Amen.

Trumpets
and Torches

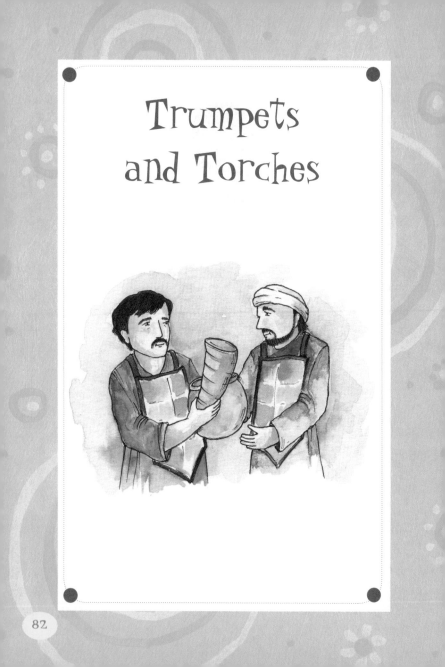

Then Gideon and his men blew their
trumpets and smashed their jars.
JUDGES 7:19 NCV

What do soldiers use to fight the enemy?
God told Gideon to use some strange things to
fight his enemy.

Gideon and his men were camped near soldiers from a land called Midian.

"I want you to have a victory," God told
Gideon. "But you will have to follow my orders
to get it."

First of all, God told Gideon that he had too
many men. Gideon told many of his soldiers to
go home. Soon there were only three hundred
men left in Gideon's army.

Gideon gave each of the men a trumpet and an
empty jar. Then he put a torch inside each jar.

"Watch me," said Gideon. "Do what I do."

The men surrounded the enemy camp. They watched Gideon. When Gideon reached the edge of the enemy camp, he blew the trumpet and broke the jar with the torches. The other men did the same.

The enemies were confused and afraid. They began fighting each other. Soon they ran away. Gideon and his men won the battle with only trumpets and torches!

Dear God, sometimes You tell me
to do things I don't understand.
But I know You love me and You
know what is best for me to do.
Amen.

Secret Strength

[Samson] said, "I have never had my hair cut, because I have been set apart to God as a Nazirite since I was born. If someone shaved my head, I would lose my strength."

JUDGES 16:17 NCV

HOW do you feel when you do something wrong? Samson did a lot of things wrong. But God gave Samson miracle power even after he had disobeyed.

God had given Samson great strength. But Samson disobeyed God. He loved a woman who did not love God.

The woman, Delilah, tried to trick Samson. She kept asking, "What is the secret of your strength?"

Finally, Samson got tired of her asking. He

said, "If my hair is cut, I will lose my strength."

When Samson fell asleep, Delilah cut his hair. He was no longer strong. The enemy took him prisoner and blinded him.

Samson was put in jail. But his hair slowly grew long again.

On the day of a great feast, the enemy brought Samson to their temple. They wanted to laugh at him.

Samson was put between the pillars of the building. Then he prayed, "God, give me strength once again so I can destroy the enemy."

Samson pushed on the pillars with all his strength. *Crash!* The building came down! God used Samson's strength to kill the enemy.

Thank You, God, for loving me
even when I do wrong things.
I need Your help to do what is
right. Help me please You, God.
Amen.

Angels All Around

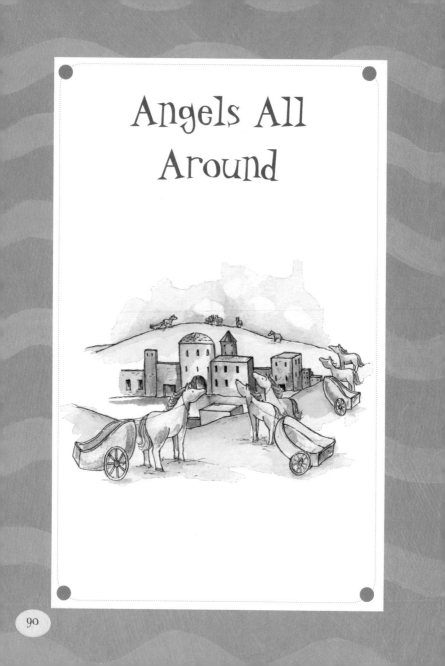

Elisha prayed, "Lord, open my servant's eyes so he can see." Then the Lord opened his eyes.

2 KINGS 6:17 NIrV

Have you ever been afraid? Elisha wasn't afraid when the enemy came to capture him. He knew that God would show him a miracle.

The king of Aram shouted at his army officers. "Who is telling the king of Israel all my secret plans?"

One of the officers said, "It's not one of us. Elisha tells the king everything you say—even your secrets."

"Then capture Elisha!" shouted the king.

The next morning Elisha's servant saw the army from Aram. "Elisha!" he shouted. "The army of Aram has surrounded the city! What are we going to do?"

"Don't be afraid," said Elisha. "Come with me."

The two men climbed up high so they could look over the city walls. Many soldiers surrounded the city.

"Don't be afraid," said Elisha. "Our army is much bigger than that army." Then Elisha prayed, "God, open my servant's eyes. Let him see."

God opened the servant's eyes. What an amazing sight! All around the city, the hills were filled with horses and chariots of fire! God's army of angels had surrounded the enemy.

Thank You, God for keeping
me safe from harm. Please give
me courage. Help me not to be
afraid, but to trust in You.
Amen.

The Dried-Up Hand

So the man of God prayed to the LORD,
and the king's arm was healed,
becoming as it was before.
1 KINGS 13:6 NCV

Have you ever told someone something they didn't like? A man of God gave a bad king a message he didn't like. Then two miracles happened.

Jeroboam was the bad king. He did not worship God.

One day a man of God went to see the king. He had a message from God.

The man of God found King Jeroboam standing by the altar. The man of God cried out, "God will send a sign to you. The altar will break into pieces. The ashes will be spilled out."

Jeroboam didn't like what the man of God

told him. "Grab him!" the angry king yelled to his servants. But when Jeroboam pointed his hand toward the man of God, his hand dried up. He couldn't move it.

Suddenly the altar broke into pieces and the ashes spilled out—just like the man of God had said.

Jeroboam looked at his wrinkled hand and said, "Pray to your God for me. Pray that my hand will be healed."

The man of God prayed. And Jeroboam's hand was healed.

Dear God, I thank You for
giving me courage. Help me
tell my friends what You want
me to say, even if they don't
want to hear it. Amen.

Enough to Eat

The birds brought Elijah bread and meat every morning and evening, and he drank water from the stream.

1 KINGS 17:6 NCV

Are you thankful for the good food your mom gives you each day? When Elijah needed food, God gave him a miracle. Elijah was thankful that he obeyed God.

King Ahab was a bad king. He would not let the people worship God. God sent Elijah to talk to him.

"I serve God but you do not obey Him, King Ahab," said Elijah. "So it will not rain until I say."

God told Elijah that He would take care of him. God said Elijah should go to a certain stream of water. "Stay here," God said. "I will give you food and water." Elijah obeyed God.

God sent birds to take care of Elijah. The birds brought bread and meat every morning and every evening. Elijah drank water from the stream.

But since there was no rain, the water in the stream soon dried up.

"You cannot stay here," God told Elijah. "Go into town. A lady there will give you food and water."

Elijah obeyed God. He knew that God would take care of him.

Thank You, God, for the
grownups who give me good food
to eat and water to drink.
I know You will always
take care of me. Amen.

Miracle Oil and Flour

"The LORD, the God of Israel, says:
'The jar of flour will not be used up and
the jug of oil will not run dry until the
day the LORD gives rain on the land.' "
1 KINGS 17:14 NIV

HOW long does the food Mom buys at the store last? God gave a woman some food that lasted for three years. What a miracle!

Elijah was hungry and thirsty. It had not rained for a long time and food was hard to find. God spoke to Elijah. "Go into town," God said. "A woman there will feed you."

When Elijah reached the village, he saw a woman gathering sticks. "Would you please bring me a cup of water and a little bread?" he asked.

The woman said sadly, "I don't have any

bread. I have only a little flour and a little oil. I will make a fire and cook one last meal for my son and me. Then we will die because we have nothing to eat."

Elijah said, "Don't be afraid. Go and cook the meal, but first make me a little loaf of bread. God promises there will always be plenty of flour and oil until He sends a rain."

The woman believed God's promise. It did not rain for three years—but she always had food to eat.

Thank You, God, for sending
rain for the food to grow.
I know I can always trust Your
promises. You are good to me
and my family. Amen.

Fire Came Down

The fire of the Lord came down.
It burned up the sacrifice.
It burned up the wood
and the stones and the soil.
It even licked up the water
in the ditch.

1 KINGS 18:38 NIrV

Do you know why we need rain? God sends rain to give us water to drink and food to eat. When it had not rained for a long time, God sent Elijah to show the people a miracle.

"You make the people pray to a false god named Baal," Elijah told King Ahab. "They no longer believe in God. I will show them the real God's power."

The people went to Mount Carmel. King Ahab and his prophets went also.

"I will show you that my God has the most power," Elijah said to the people.

Then Elijah said to the prophets. "Make an offering and pray to your false god, Baal. I will make an offering and pray to my God. Whoever answers by sending fire down will be the most powerful."

The prophets made an offering and prayed. Nothing happened. They prayed some more. Nothing happened.

Elijah made an offering and prayed. God sent fire down on the offering. The fire burned up the offering. The people believed in Elijah's God and the rain began.

Dear God, I thank You for sending rain to give me water to drink and food to eat. You are a powerful God. You are my God. Amen.

Carried Away

As they were walking and talking,
a chariot and horses of fire appeared
and separated Elijah from Elisha.
Then Elijah went up to
heaven in a whirlwind.

2 KINGS 2:11 NCV

Are you afraid when strong winds bend the trees? God used a whirlwind and a chariot of fire with horses to take Elijah to heaven. Do you think he was afraid?

One day, Elijah talked to Elisha. "God is taking me to heaven soon. Please stay here. God wants me to go to the Jordan River now."

Elisha did not understand. "Don't leave me!" Elisha said. "I will go, too."

At the Jordan River, Elijah rolled up his coat and hit the water with it. The water stopped flowing. They walked across on dry ground.

Elijah asked, "Is there anything I can do for you before I go, Elisha?"

"I want to do God's work like you have done," Elisha said.

"If you see me when I go, it will happen," Elijah said.

As Elijah and Elisha walked along, a chariot of fire with horses came down from heaven. It carried Elijah away in a whirlwind. Elisha saw him go and knew that he would do God's work.

Dear God, sometimes I'm like
Elisha. I don't understand all
that is happening around me.
But help me, God, always to do
what pleases You. Amen.

A Dip in the River

So Naaman went down and dipped in the Jordan seven times, just as Elisha had said. Then his skin became new again, like the skin of a child. And he was clean.

2 KINGS 5:14 NCV

When you are sick, do you do what the doctor tells you to do to become well? Naaman needed a miracle if he wanted to be well again.

Naaman was a commander in the army. One day, Naaman became sick. He was covered with sores. Naaman was sad.

A young girl who helped Naaman's wife said, "Naaman needs to go see Elisha. He can make him well again."

Naaman's helpers got his horses and chariot ready for the trip. *Clippity-clop, clippity-clop* went the horses' feet. *Rumble, rumble* went the chariot wheels.

Naaman came to Elisha's house. "Go dip in the Jordan River seven times and you will be well," said Elisha's helper.

Naaman went to the Jordan River. He dipped one, two, three times, and nothing happened. He dipped four, five, six times, and nothing happened. But when Naaman dipped into the river the seventh time, he came out of the water with clean skin. His sores were gone.

Naaman knew Elisha's God had given him a miracle to make him well again.

Thank You, God, for being near
me and taking care of me today.
I thank You for doctors who
help me to get well when
I am sick. Amen.

The Heavy Axe Floats

Elisha asked, "Where did it fall?"
The man showed him the place.
Then Elisha cut down a stick and
threw it into the water, and it
made the iron head float.

2 KINGS 6:6 NCV

Have you ever thrown rocks into the

water? Do they float or sink? One time, a man
dropped a heavy axe into the deep water. He
needed a miracle to get it out.

A group of people said to Elisha, "This place
is too small for us. Let's move to the Jordan River
and build a bigger place to worship."

Elisha said, "Go!"

"Please come with us," said one of the
men.

When Elisha and the people arrived at the

Jordan River, the men began cutting trees. *Chop, chop, chop!* went the axes. Trees were falling all around them.

"Oh no!" cried one man. "My axe fell into the deep river. How can I get it out?"

The man showed Elisha where the axe had fallen. Elisha knew God would show him what to do. So Elisha cut a stick and threw it into the water.

Down went the stick. Up came the heavy axe. It floated on the water. The man reached down and took the heavy axe out of the water.

Dear God, I know You can do
things that seem impossible. You
are a great and powerful God.
Help me to remember You
can do all things. Amen.

Three Men Obeyed God

"But look!" [the king] said. "I see four men, walking around freely in the fire, completely unharmed! And the fourth man looks like a son of the gods!"

DANIEL 3:25 MSG

Have you ever burned your finger on something hot? One time, three men were thrown into a big fire—but a miracle kept them safe.

King Nebuchadnezzar made a giant statue. The king called together all the people of the land. He told them, "When you hear the music, bow down to the statue. Anyone who does not bow down will be thrown into a fiery furnace."

Shadrach, Meshach, and Abednego came to the meeting. But they would not bow down to the statue. They worshipped only God.

King Nebuchadnezzar was angry because the men would not obey him. He had them thrown into the furnace.

When the king looked into the furnace, he was surprised. He said, "I see four men walking in the fire. The fourth is like a god!"

So the king shouted, "Shadrach, Meshach, and Abednego, come out!"

The three men came out. The fire had not burned them. Everyone was surprised.

King Nebuchadnezzar said, "You have a great God. He kept you safe in the fire."

Dear God, I thank You for
keeping me safe when there is
danger around me. You are the
only true God. I will worship
only You. Amen.

Handwriting on the Wall

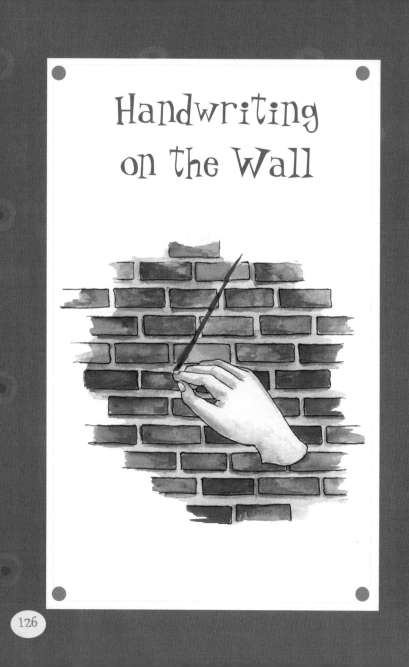

Suddenly the fingers of a human hand appeared and wrote on the plaster of the wall, near the lampstand in the royal palace. The king watched the hand as it wrote.

Have you ever gotten in trouble for writing on a wall? God used a hand to write a message on a palace wall. He wanted to get the king's attention—and it worked!

King Belshazzar gave a party to show people how important he was. He served wine in golden cups that had been stolen from God's temple. The king and his people worshipped idols made of gold, silver, and wood.

Suddenly, in the middle of the party, a strange hand appeared. It began writing on the wall of the palace. King Belshazzar was frightened.

"Bring the wise men," shouted the king. They came and looked at the message. But they could not read it.

The queen heard the king's voice and came into the room. She said. "Daniel can tell you the meaning of this message."

Daniel was brought before the king. When he looked at the writing, he said, "God is unhappy because you have disobeyed Him. The message says that you will no longer be king."

That night, the message came true. A new king took over the country.

Dear God, sometimes I get in trouble for doing the wrong things. I thank You for the Bible that shows me how to obey. Amen.

In the Lions' Den

> "My God sent his angel. And his angel
> shut the mouths of the lions.
> They haven't hurt me at all."
>
> DANIEL 6:22 NIrV

Do you like to hear lions roar at the zoo? One time, God shut some lions' mouths so they couldn't roar—or eat Daniel.

Some bad men wanted to hurt Daniel because he prayed to God. So they tricked the king into making a new rule.

"Everyone must bow down to me," the king told the people. "If you do not, you will be thrown into the lions' den."

The next day, those bad men watched Daniel. They saw him praying. But he didn't bow to the king.

The men ran to the king. "You made a

rule," they tattled. "You must obey the rule. Daniel was praying to God. Throw him into the lions' den."

The king was sad, but he had to obey his own rule. Daniel was thrown into the lions' den.

R–r–roar! The lions were hungry. But Daniel knew God would take care of him. And God did just that! God sent an angel to shut the lions' mouths.

When the king checked on Daniel the next day, he found that Daniel's God had kept him safe.

Dear God, I like spending time
talking with You every day.
I thank You for keeping me safe.
You are always good to me.
Amen.

Jonah and the Fish

The Lord gave the fish a command.
And it spit Jonah up onto dry land.
JONAH 2:10 NIrV

Have you ever gone fishing and caught a big one? Have you ever heard of a fish catching a man? That happened one time!

"Jonah," God said, "go to the city of Nineveh. Tell the people about Me."

Jonah didn't obey God. He got on a boat and sailed the other way.

So God sent a big storm. The waves crashed! The boat rocked! Even the strong sailors were afraid!

Jonah knew God had sent the storm because he had disobeyed. So Jonah said, "Throw me into the water. Then the storm will stop."

One, two, THREE! The sailors threw Jonah

into the water. The waves stopped crashing. The boat stopped rocking.

Then God sent a big fish. The fish opened its mouth. *Whoosh!* Jonah went into the fish's mouth!

Jonah prayed. "I'm sorry, God. Forgive me for running away. I will go and tell the people about You."

After three days, the fish began to cough. *AACK!* The fish coughed Jonah onto the beach.

God talked to Jonah again. He said, "Go!" This time, Jonah obeyed.

Dear God, please give me courage to tell my friends about You. Help me not to be afraid, but excited about sharing the stories in the Bible with them. Amen.

Star of Bethlehem

When they saw the star, they rejoiced
with exceeding great joy.
MATTHEW 2:10 KJV

Do you like to look at the stars? Can you find certain stars in the sky? God used a bright star to tell the wise men about the baby Jesus.

In a far country, very smart men studied the stars. One night, they saw a new star that was brighter than the others.

"Let's follow this star," said one of the wise men. "It will lead us to a new king."

For many days and nights, the wise men followed the star. When they came to Bethlehem, they went to see King Herod.

"Where is the new king?" asked the wise men. "We have seen his star in the east and have come to worship him."

King Herod was surprised. "When you find the young child, tell me." Herod said he wanted to worship Jesus, too. But he really wanted to get rid of anyone who might take his place.

Soon the wise men saw the star again. It was over the house where Jesus and His parents lived. There they found Jesus and gave Him gifts—gold, frankincense, and myrrh. The wise men were happy to worship Jesus.

Thank You, God, for sending
Your Son, Jesus. Just like the
wise men, I am happy when
I worship Jesus. My gift to
Jesus is myself. Amen.

A Special Promise

[Mary] gave birth to her first baby. It was a boy. She wrapped him in large strips of cloth. Then she placed him in a manger. There was no room for them in the inn.

LUKE 2:7 NIrV

Has someone ever made you a promise? A promise is something you say you will do. Then you should do that. In the Bible, God made a special promise to send His Son.

One day, an angel stood beside Mary. "Don't be afraid," the angel said. "God has chosen you to be the mother of a special baby. You will name the baby Jesus. This special baby will be God's Son!" Mary was glad to hear this promise.

Soon it came time for Mary and Joseph, her husband, to go to Bethlehem. *Clippety-clop, clippety-clop!* Mary rode on the donkey. Joseph walked beside her. It was a long trip and Mary was tired.

Finally they got to Bethlehem. The town was full of people. There was no place for them to sleep. So Mary and Joseph went to a stable where animals were kept.

In the nighttime, the baby Jesus was born. Mary wrapped the baby in warm clothes. She laid Jesus on soft hay in the manger. Mary and Joseph took care of this special baby that God had promised.

Dear God, I thank You for keeping Your special promise. Thank You for sending Your Son, Jesus. Help me to keep all of the promises that I make. Amen.

Jesus Helped at a Wedding

> The person in charge tasted the water
> that had been turned into wine.
>
> JOHN 2:9 NIrV

Have you ever been to a wedding? Do you remember how long the wedding and party lasted? Weddings and parties where Jesus lived lasted several days. Jesus helped at a wedding by performing His first miracle.

Jesus and his helpers were guests at a wedding feast. Jesus' mother was also at the party. She noticed the wine had been used up. So she said to Jesus, "They are out of wine."

Nearby, there were six large, stone water pots. "Fill the pots with water," Jesus told the servants. The servants filled the pots to the top. Then Jesus said, "Now take some out and give it to the person in charge of the feast."

The servants did as Jesus asked. When the person in charge of the feast tasted the drink, he was surprised. He called the bridegroom and said, "Most people serve their best wine first, but you have saved the best until last."

Jesus had turned water into wine. It was the first of many miracles that Jesus did.

Dear God, I thank You for
sending Jesus to be my example.
He did good things for others.
I want to be like Him and
help others. Amen.

A Happy Day for a Sick Man

Take up your bed and walk.

At once the man was healed. He picked up his mat and walked.

JOHN 5:9 NIrV

Are you sad when you see someone who is sick? Do you think Jesus was sad to see sick people? He made one sick man very happy by performing a miracle on him.

One day, Jesus walked near the pool of Bethesda. There were many sick people near the water. They believed that when the water moved, the first person to get into the pool would be healed.

When Jesus visited the pool, he saw a sick man who had tried many times to get into the pool first. The man couldn't walk. He just lay on the mat and stared at the water.

Jesus walked over to the man and asked,

"Would you like to be healed?"

"Sir," said the man, "I have no one to put me into the pool at the right time."

Then Jesus told him to do a surprising thing. "Get up," Jesus said. "Take up your bed and walk."

This man hadn't walked for many years. But he believed Jesus and immediately jumped to his feet. He picked up his bed. He could walk!

Dear Jesus, I thank You for
helping people to get well
and making them happy. Show
me what I can do to make
people happy, too. Amen.

A Hole in the Roof

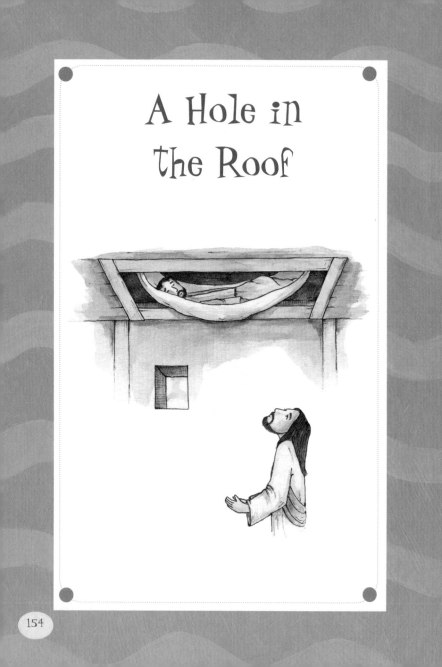

> At once the man stood up
> before them, picked up his mat,
> and went home, praising God.
> LUKE 5:25 NCV

What would you do if you couldn't find a place to sit at church? Something like that happened to some men when they took their friend to see Jesus.

Many people crowded into a house to hear Jesus teach. Four men were carrying a friend on a mat. He could not walk. The four men wanted Jesus to heal their friend, but they couldn't get into the crowded house. What could they do?

Before long, the man on the mat was going *up, up, up!* His friends had tied a rope to each corner of the mat. The man was lifted to the flat roof of the house. *Rip! Crash!* The four men began to tear the roof apart. They lowered their friend down through a hole in the roof. He came down in the middle of the people, right in front of Jesus.

Jesus knew the man's friends wanted the man to be made well. So Jesus said to the man, "You are forgiven. Get up. Take your mat and go home."

At once, the man jumped up. He grabbed his mat and ran home praising God.

Dear God, I thank You for the
grownups who take me to church.
I thank You for my teachers who
tell me the stories about Jesus.
Amen.

The Man Who Couldn't Hear

And it happened.
The man's hearing was clear
and his speech plain—just like that.

MARK 7:35 MSG

Have you ever wondered what it would be like not to hear or speak? You couldn't enjoy the birds singing or your mom reading you a story. You couldn't talk to your friends. When Jesus touched a man who couldn't hear or speak, a miracle happened.

One day, some people came to Jesus with a man who was deaf and could not talk. They begged Jesus to put His hands on the man and heal him.

Jesus took the man away from the crowd to a quiet place. Jesus put His fingers in the deaf man's ears. Next Jesus spit and touched the man's tongue. Then Jesus looked up to heaven and sighed. He said to the man, "Be opened."

At that very moment, the man's ears were opened so he could hear. And the man could speak plainly. How excited he must have been! The people who knew him were amazed. "Jesus does everything well," they said. "He makes the deaf hear and those who can't talk, He makes able to speak."

Thank You, God, for my ears so I can hear and my tongue that helps me talk. Help me to listen and say only the things that are pleasing to You. Amen.

The Man Who Couldn't See

"Go," [Jesus] told him.
"Wash in the Pool of Siloam."
Siloam means Sent.
So the man went and washed.
And he came home able to see.

JOHN 9:7 NIrV

Have you ever wondered how it would feel to be blind? Close your eyes and feel around. Let someone help you walk across the room. How do you feel? Jesus used a miracle to help a man born blind to see.

As Jesus walked along a road, He saw a man who had been blind all his life.

Some of the people asked Jesus, "Is this man blind because he did something wrong? Or did his parents do something wrong?"

Jesus answered, "This man did nothing

wrong. His parents did nothing wrong. It happened so that God's power could be shown."

Then Jesus spit on the ground. He made some mud with the spit. Then he put the mud on the man's eyes.

"Go," Jesus told him. "Wash in the Pool of Siloam."

The man went to the pool and washed. When he did, he could see.

The people asked, "Is this the same man who was blind?"

The man answered, "I am the man. Jesus healed my eyes."

Dear God, I thank You for
giving me eyes to see the things
around me. Help me see only
the good and right things
that please You. Amen.

Jesus Heals a Man's Hand

[Jesus] said to the man,
"Stretch out your hand."
He stretched it out,
and his hand was as good as new.

MARK 3:5 NIrV

Do you always follow the rules that are pleasing to God? Jesus showed people how to please God by following His rules.

Jesus was at church on a special day called the Sabbath. The church leaders were watching people as they worshipped God. They made sure God's rules were followed—but they had also made rules of their own. The leaders did not like Jesus. They didn't want people to believe that Jesus was God's Son. They tried to make people think Jesus disobeyed God.

Jesus saw a man with a crippled hand. He

said to the man, "Stand up in front of everyone." Then Jesus asked the people, "Is it better to do good or to do bad on the Sabbath?" No one answered.

Jesus was angry and sad. He knew the leaders did not love the man or God—they only loved their rules. Jesus looked at the leaders. Then he looked at the man with the crippled hand. "Stretch out your hand," Jesus said. The man stretched out his hand, and it was healed.

Dear God, I know Your rules
are good. Help me follow rules
that are pleasing to You. Help
me to be like Jesus and do good
things every day. Amen.

Jesus Calms
the Storm

The followers went to Jesus and woke him, saying, "Master! Master! We will drown!" Jesus got up and gave a command to the wind and the waves. They stopped, and it became calm.

LUKE 8:24 NCV

Are you afraid when there's a bad storm? Who helps you when you're afraid? Jesus helped His friends when they were afraid. He showed them a miracle.

"Let's go to the other side of the lake," Jesus once said to His friends. They got in their boat and set out across the lake.

Rock, rock, rock! The water gently rocked the boat. Jesus fell asleep.

Whoo-oo, whoo-oo! Suddenly the wind began to blow.

Big, dark clouds gathered in the sky. A bad storm was coming.

Flash! Flash! went the lightning. *Boom, boom!* went the thunder. *Splash, splash!* went the waves against the boat. Water came into the boat.

Jesus's friends were afraid. They woke Jesus and said, "Master, Master! We are going to drown!"

Jesus got up and spoke to the wind and water. The wind stopped blowing. The lightning stopped flashing. The thunder stopped booming. The waves stopped splashing into the boat. The dark clouds went away. The gentle waves began to rock the boat again.

Dear God, sometimes I'm afraid
when there is a storm. Help me
to trust You when I am afraid.
You know how to keep me safe.
Amen.

Walking on Water

> "Come," [Jesus] said. Then Peter got down out of the boat, walked on the water and came toward Jesus.
> MATTHEW 14:29 NIV

What happens to you when you jump into a lake? Do you start to sink in the water? Peter was surprised when he got out of a boat and didn't sink.

Jesus had been teaching all day. He was tired. He wanted to be alone for a while, so He sent His helpers to the other side of the sea.

Suddenly, the wind began to blow. *Whoo-oo!* The waves got bigger. *Splash! Splash!*

Early in the morning, Jesus went out to the helpers. He was walking on the water! When the helpers saw Him, they yelled, "It's a ghost!" They were afraid.

"It's Me," Jesus said. "Don't be afraid."

Peter said, "Lord, if it's really You, tell me to come to You on the water."

"Come," said Jesus.

Peter got out of the boat and walked on the water to Jesus!

But then Peter saw the big waves. He saw how hard the wind was blowing. He was afraid and began to sink. "Lord, save me!" he cried out.

Jesus caught Peter's hand and helped him into the boat.

Dear Jesus, You know how to keep me safe. I thank You for taking care of me and being with me. Give me courage when I'm afraid. Amen.

A Lunch to Share

Then Jesus took the bread and, having given thanks, gave it to those who were seated. He did the same with the fish. All ate as much as they wanted.

JOHN 6:11 MSG

What would happen if you were having a picnic and lots of people came to join you? Would you have enough food for everyone? One time, Jesus used a miracle to feed a huge, hungry crowd.

Many people followed Jesus up a mountainside. Jesus healed the sick. He told them about God. Soon evening came and the people were hungry.

Jesus told one of His helpers, "Give the people something to eat."

Philip said, "We don't have any food."

Another helper named Andrew said, "There is a boy here who has a lunch with five small bread loaves and two fish."

"Bring the loaves and fish to Me," Jesus said. "Tell the people to sit down on the grass."

Jesus held up the bread and fish. He thanked God for the food. Then He broke the food into pieces. Jesus gave the food to the people. They ate until everyone had enough.

The helpers gathered up the food that was not eaten. There were twelve basketfuls left. What a miracle!

Dear God, I thank You for the
Bible stories about Jesus.
I know those stories are true.
Help me to share the stories
about Jesus with my friends.
Amen.

A Son Is Made Well

And as he was going down,
his servants met him,
and told him, saying,
Thy son liveth.

Who helps you when you're sick? Your mom or dad probably take you to the doctor. They also pray for you to get well. Jesus made a sick boy well without even seeing him.

An important official met Jesus as He was walking into a city. The official had heard about Jesus and how He could heal people. The official had a sick son in another town. He wanted Jesus to help.

"Please, Jesus," the official begged, "come heal my son."

"Until you and the people see a miracle, you

will not believe in Me," Jesus said.

The official said to Jesus again, "Come with me before my son dies."

Jesus replied, "Go home. Your son will live."

The official believed what Jesus said and left for home. On the way, his servants met him. They told him his son was well.

"What time did he get well?" asked the official.

When they told him the time, the officer knew that was the exact time Jesus said his son would live.

Dear Jesus, sometimes doctors
help me get well. But I know
that You always help me when
I am sick. I thank You for
taking care of me. Amen.

At Peter's House

When the sun went down, the people
brought those who were sick to Jesus.
Putting his hands on each sick person,
he healed every one of them.

LUKE 4:40 NCV

Have you ever had a friend over but were
too tired to play? Jesus got tired, too—but He
still performed miracles for people who needed
them.

All day long, Jesus had been telling people
about God. He was tired, so He went to Peter's
house to rest. He found Peter's mother-in-law
very sick.

Jesus went to her bedside and touched her.
Her fever went away. She was well and strong
again!

Neighbors had seen Jesus go into Peter's

house. They had heard that He had healed Peter's mother-in-law. Soon everyone in the city had heard the news. People hurried to Peter's house to see Jesus.

Suddenly, Peter heard noises outside his door. When he looked outside, he was surprised. "Look at all the people!" he said. "They have come to find Jesus."

Jesus looked out and saw the people. "I cannot turn them away," He said. "They need me."

Jesus stepped outside. He put his hands on the sick and healed them. He talked with those who were lonely. Jesus cared for the people.

Dear God, I thank You for sending Your Son, Jesus, to be with us. He is my friend. Help me to be like Jesus and care for others. Amen.

Jesus Showed That He Cared

When he had said this,
Jesus called in a loud voice,
"Lazarus, come out!"
The dead man came out.

JOHN 11:43–44 NIV

Have you known someone who has died? Did that make you sad? Mary and Martha were sad when their brother died. But Jesus performed a miracle to make them happy again.

Lazarus was very sick. Mary and Martha sent a message to Jesus, telling Him, "Your friend Lazarus is sick."

Jesus stayed where He was for two more days. Lazarus died before Jesus got to His friend's house.

When Jesus arrived, Martha ran out to meet Him. She said, "Jesus, if you had been here,

Lazarus would not have died. You could have made him well."

Jesus said, "You brother will live again."

"I know he will live in heaven," said Martha.

Jesus asked, "Do you believe in Me?"

Martha answered, "Yes, Lord! I do believe."

Then Mary and Martha took Jesus to the place where Lazarus was buried.

Jesus said, "Take the stone away from the grave."

After Jesus prayed to God, He called, "Lazarus, come out!"

Lazarus, who had been dead, walked out of the grave. Mary and Martha were happy that Jesus cared for them.

Dear God, I thank You for
taking care of me when I'm sad—
even when someone I love dies.
I know You can make me happy
again, God. Amen.

"Little Girl, Get Up!"

Immediately the girl stood up
and walked around
(she was twelve years old).
At this they were
completely astonished.

MARK 5:42 NIV

When you are sick, do you believe Jesus can make you well? Jairus believed that Jesus could do a miracle—even when he was told his daughter had died.

As Jesus stepped off a boat, people gathered around Him. Jairus, a leader at church, hurried through the crowd to see Jesus. He had heard that Jesus could heal sick people.

When Jairus reached Jesus, he fell at His feet. "Jesus, my daughter is only twelve years old and dying," said Jairus. "Please come to my house and put your hands on her. I know if You touch her, she will get well."

Jesus went with Jairus. On the way to the house, they met some men. "It's too late," they said. "Your daughter is dead. You don't need Jesus."

"Don't be afraid," said Jesus to Jairus. "Just keep believing in Me."

When they got to Jairus's house, Jesus went into the room where the dead girl lay. He took her hand. "Little girl, get up!" said Jesus.

Quickly, the little girl stood up and walked around. The people were amazed!

Thank You, Jesus, for making
me well when I am sick. Help me
to remember to pray for Your
help when my family and
friends are sick. Amen.

Ten Men Healed

When Jesus saw the men, he said,
"Go and show yourselves to the priests."
As the ten men were going,
they were healed.
LUKE 17:14 NCV

Have you ever given something special to someone who didn't say "thank you"? How did that make you feel? Jesus once healed some men who were sick. Do you think they said "thank you"?

As Jesus walked toward town one day, ten men called out. "Jesus, have pity on us!"

Jesus knew the men had sores on their bodies. They couldn't live in town because they might give their families and neighbors the disease.

The ten men heard that Jesus had made many people well. They wanted Him to make them well, too.

Jesus said to them, "Go and show yourselves to the priest at the temple."

Though the men still had sores, they did what Jesus told them. They ran straight for the priest. And as they went, they were healed! Their sores were gone. Their skin was soft again.

Jesus watched the men running away. But suddenly, one man stopped. He turned around and shouted. "Praise God!" Then he ran back and fell at Jesus' feet. "Thank You for making me well," he said.

Dear Jesus, I thank You for the wonderful things You do for me. Help me to say "thank you" to others who do things for me, too. Amen.

So Many Fish

When the fishermen did as Jesus told them, they caught so many fish that the nets began to break.

LUKE 5:6 NCV

Do you like to go fishing? Have you ever gone fishing and caught nothing? That's what happened to some fishermen until Jesus came along. Then everything changed.

One day, Jesus stood by the Sea of Galilee. People were crowded around Him, listening to His teaching. When Jesus saw two boats by the shore, He got into the boat that belonged to Simon.

"Go out away from the shore," Jesus told Simon. Then Jesus sat down in the boat to teach the people.

Later, Jesus said to Simon, "Go out into the

deep water. Let the nets down so you can catch some fish."

"But Jesus, we've fished all night and caught nothing," Simon answered. "But we will do what You say."

Simon and the fishermen did what Jesus told them. They were surprised when they pulled up their nets full of fish. There were so many fish, the nets began to break.

"Come help us!" yelled Simon to the fishermen in the other boat.

The fishermen came and helped. They had so many fish that they filled both boats!

Thank You, God, for sometimes giving me more than I really need. You are so good to me. Help me to share what I have with others. Amen.

Touching
the Hem

Jesus said to her, "Dear woman,
you are made well because you believed.
Go in peace; be healed of your disease."

MARK 5:34 NCV

How does it feel to be in a large crowd?
Sometimes people bump into you on every side.
That's how it was when Jesus was in a large
crowd. But He still felt someone special touching him.

A large crowd of people followed Jesus. The
people were pushing very close to Him.

One was a woman who had been sick for
twelve years. She had been to many doctors,
but none could make her well. When she heard
about Jesus, she wanted to see Him.

If I could only touch Him, the sick woman
thought. *I would be healed.*

Slowly, the woman moved closer. Finally, she reached out and touched Jesus's coat. Something wonderful happened—she felt her body healed of her disease!

Jesus turned and looked at the crowd. "Who touched Me?" He asked.

The woman came and fell at Jesus' feet. She was shaking with fear. "I touched You," she said.

"Woman, you were made well because you believed in Me," Jesus told her. "You are healed of your disease."

Thank You, Jesus, for keeping me well. When my friends or family members are sick, help me to remember to pray for them. You can make them well, too. Amen.

Bartimaeus Can See

"Go," said Jesus.
"Your faith has healed you."
Right away he could see.
And he followed Jesus along the road.
MARK 10:52 NIrV

Close your eyes. Don't peek! Put your arms out and move them around. Do you feel anything? Take a deep breath. Do you smell anything? Listen! Do you hear anything? Bartimaeus could feel and smell things around him. He could hear people talking. But he couldn't see anything.

One day, while Bartimaeus sat by the road, he heard people shouting. "Jesus is coming!" they said.

Bartimaeus began to shout, too. "Jesus! Son of David! Have mercy on me!"

The people told him to be quiet. But he shouted even louder, "Jesus! Son of David! Have mercy on me!"

Jesus stopped and said, "Call him."

The people called to Bartimaeus, "Get up! Jesus is calling you."

Bartimaeus threw his coat off and jumped to his feet. He moved toward Jesus.

"What do you want Me to do for you?" asked Jesus.

"I want to be able to see," said the blind man.

"Go," said Jesus. "Believing in Me has healed you."

Right then, Bartimaeus could see everything around him. "I can see," he said. And he followed Jesus down the road.

Dear God, I thank You for
giving me eyes to see the beautiful world around me. Help me to
be thankful for miracles—big
ones and small ones. Amen.

Then [Jesus] put his hands on her.
Right away she stood up straight
and praised God.
LUKE 13:13 NIrV

Do you know people who need a cane to help them walk? Sometimes people who've hurt their backs need a cane. One time, Jesus performed a miracle for a woman with a crooked back.

Jesus was teaching at the church. Many people were there. They wanted to hear what He was saying.

Tap, tap, tap! Jesus looked up. He saw a woman walking along the street toward the church.

For many years, the woman had not been able to stand up straight. Her back was so crooked that she bent over when she walked. *Shuffle,*

shuffle, shuffle! She moved down the street.

Tap, tap, tap! The woman used the cane to climb the steps of the church. She wanted to hear the words that Jesus said, too.

When Jesus saw the woman, He said, "Woman, come here. I am going to make you well."

Jesus put His hands on her. Suddenly, the woman's back became strong. She stood up straight. She didn't need her cane anymore. And she began praising God.

Dear God, You can heal people and make them well. Please help my friends and relatives who are weak. You are a great God. Amen.

Jesus Is Alive!

> He is not here: for he is risen,
> as he said. Come, see the place
> where the Lord lay.
>
> MATTHEW 28:6 KJV

What do you look like when you feel sad? When you feel happy? Jesus's friends were sad—but then they heard some good news that made them happy.

One day, Jesus told his friends, "Some people are going to kill Me." His friends were very sad. But Jesus knew this was part of God's plan.

A few days later, Jesus died on the cross. His friends took Jesus's body and put it in a tomb. A huge rock was rolled in front of the tomb.

After Jesus had been in the tomb three days, two of His friends, Mary Magdalene and Mary, came to the tomb. *Tremble, tremble!* The ground began to shake. An angel rolled the rock back from the tomb.

"Don't be afraid," the angel told the women. "I know you are looking for Jesus. But He is not here. He is risen! Go tell His helpers that Jesus is alive!"

The women hurried to tell Jesus' helpers the good news. A sad day turned into a happy day—because Jesus is alive!

Jesus, You make each day
special. I am so happy that You
are alive! I want to tell my
friends about You so they will
be happy, too. Amen.

Going to Heaven

After Jesus said this,
he was taken up to heaven.
They watched until a cloud
hid him from their sight.

ACTS 1:9 NIrV

Did you know that someday Jesus will return to earth? He will take us to heaven to be with Him. Won't that be a happy time? But until then, Jesus gave us a job.

After Jesus rose from the tomb, His friends were so happy. Jesus was alive! Jesus stayed with His friends for many days.

Then came the time for Jesus to go to heaven. He walked with His friends out in the country.

Jesus said to His friends, "Remember that I am always with you. I will watch over you and take care of you. Someday I will come back, and we will be together in heaven."

Jesus wanted them to know that He would always be with them—even though they couldn't see Him with their eyes. "After I'm gone," Jesus said, "go and tell people everywhere that I love them."

Then Jesus rose *up, up UP!* He went right into the clouds. Jesus' friends were surprised! But they remembered His promise that He would come back.

Dear Jesus, I thank You for
promising that You will return
and take me to heaven. I want
my family and friends to know
about Your promise, too. Amen.

Strange Words

"But we hear them telling in our own languages about the great things God has done!"

ACTS 2:11 NCV

Have you ever heard people speaking another language? Could you understand what they were saying? A miracle happened when Jesus' friends wanted to tell people from other countries about Jesus.

Before Jesus went to heaven, He told his friends to go everywhere in the world and tell people about Him.

"People will not understand us," said Jesus' friends.

"I will send you a Helper," said Jesus. "Wait for the Helper."

Jesus' friends stayed together in a room.

Suddenly, there was a noise. *Whoosh! Whoosh!* It sounded like the wind. Then they saw a flash like fire. Jesus' friends began to say strange words. They had never said those words before!

Many people from faraway countries were in the city. They heard about what was happening. Jesus' friends talked to the people in their own languages. How surprised everyone was!

"What is happening?" someone asked.

"God sent us a Helper called the Holy Spirit," said Peter. "That is why we can talk so you can understand. God wanted the whole world to hear about Jesus."

Dear God, I am glad for people
who help me know about Jesus.
He is my best friend.
Please help me tell others that
Jesus loves them, too. Amen.

A Different Way

"Now get up and go into the city.
There you will be told
what you must do."
ACTS 9:6 NIrV

Have you ever had to take a different road because your way was blocked? God once led a man named Saul in a different direction, too.

Saul walked down a dusty road. He was planning to capture all the people he could find who believed in Jesus. Saul didn't like people who believed in Jesus.

Suddenly, a bright light flashed around Saul. He and his men fell to the ground. Saul couldn't see! The light had blinded him.

Then he heard a voice. "Saul! Why are you hurting Me?"

"Who are You, Lord?" asked Saul.

"I am Jesus, the one you are trying to hurt," Jesus answered. "Get up and go to the city. Someone there will tell you what to do."

Saul stood up, but he couldn't see anything. His men took his hands and led him into the city. There a man named Ananias came to Saul.

"Jesus sent me," said Ananias, who put his hands on Saul.

Immediately Saul could see. He changed direction. Now Saul believed in Jesus.

Dear Jesus, I love You—and
I thank You for loving me.
Help me to obey You
and to tell other people that
You love them, too. Amen.

An Angel Helps Peter

Suddenly an angel of the Lord appeared. A light shone in the prison cell. The angel struck Peter on his side. Peter woke up. "Quick!" the angel said. "Get up!"

ACTS 12:7 NIrV

Would you be afraid if you were locked in a room and couldn't get out? When Peter was locked in a prison cell, God sent him a miracle.

King Herod did not want Peter preaching about Jesus. So he put Peter in jail. The guards placed heavy chains on Peter's wrists. Guards stood on each side of Peter and guards stood just outside the prison door. They did not want Peter to escape.

One night, while Peter was sleeping, an angel

came into the prison. Suddenly, a bright light shone in the darkness.

"Hurry!" said the angel, shaking Peter. "Get up!"

The chains fell from Peter's wrists.

"Put on your shoes and your coat," said the angel. "Follow me."

Peter followed the angel as they walked past the guards. When Peter and the angel got to a locked iron gate, God caused it to open. Peter and the angel walked down the street. Then the angel left Peter standing alone.

Peter said to himself, "God sent an angel to help me get out of the prison!"

Dear God, You know how to keep
me safe. Help me trust You when
I'm afraid and need help. I know
You can do all things. Amen.

A Powerful Earthquake

Then, without warning, a huge
earthquake! The jailhouse tottered,
every door flew open,
all the prisoners were loose.
ACTS 16:26 MSG

Have you ever felt a very strong storm shake your house? Paul and Silas felt a powerful earthquake while in prison. A strange miracle was happening to them.

Paul and Silas were telling people about Jesus. Some of the people were glad to hear what they said.

But some of the people did not want to hear them. "Put them in jail!" they shouted.

The jailer put Paul and Silas in a dark cell. He put strong chains on their hands and feet.

Paul and Silas began praying and singing.

They were happy praising God.

Suddenly, everything shook! *Bang! Bang! Crash!* It was an earthquake! All the doors in the prison opened.

Clink! Clink! The chains fell from Paul's and Silas's hands and feet.

The noise woke the jailer. He was afraid. He tried to kill himself.

Paul shouted, "Don't hurt yourself. We're all here!"

The jailer was happy the prisoners were still there. When he took Paul and Silas home with him, they told him about Jesus. The jailer and his family believed in Jesus.

Dear God, I thank You for
keeping me safe when confusing
things happen around me. Help
me to remember that You
are always near. Amen.

A Crippled Man Walks

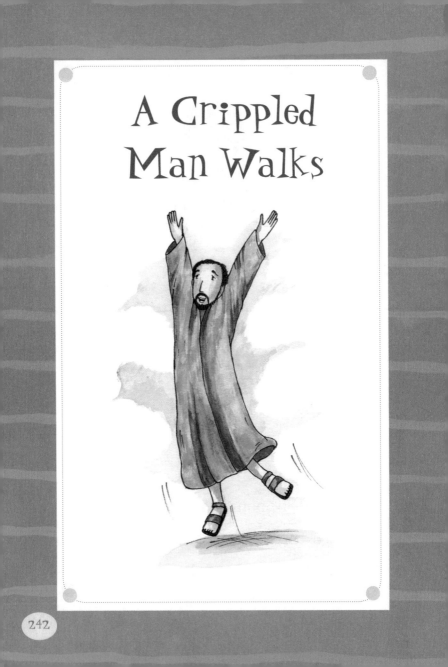

[Paul] called out, "Stand up on your feet!" At that, the man jumped up and began to walk.

ACTS 14:10 NIV

Can you wiggle your toes? Tap your feet? Jump up and down? Paul helped a man who couldn't use his feet at all.

Paul and his friend Barnabas traveled together. They used their feet to walk from town to town. In every town, they told people about Jesus. They helped people who were sick. Many people believed that Jesus was God's Son.

Paul and Barnabas came to a town called Lystra. They told the people there about Jesus, God's Son. Paul and Barnabas told the people that God loved them. They told people how Jesus could heal them.

As Paul talked, he looked at one man in the crowd. This man had never walked in his whole life. His feet didn't work. The man looked back at Paul. Paul could see that the man believed God could help him.

Paul said to the man, "Stand up on your feet!"

The man jumped to his feet. He began to walk. He jumped up and down. His feet were well! God gave the man a great healing.

Thank You, God, for strong feet
for walking and jumping. Help
me to use my feet to walk to my
friends' houses—and tell them
about Jesus. Amen.

The Story of
Eutychus

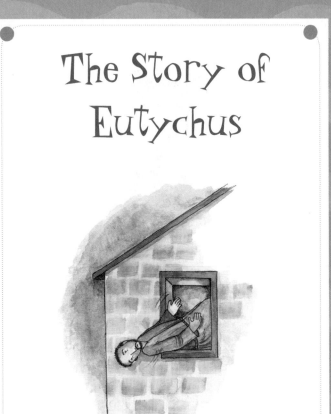

Paul went down, threw himself on the
young man and put his arms around
him. "Don't be alarmed,"
he said. "He's alive!"

ACTS 20:10 NIV

Have you ever fallen asleep at church? Eutychus fell asleep at church—and out the church window. Then God sent a miracle to help the young man.

On the first day of the week, people gathered to worship God. Paul spoke to the people. He was going to leave the next day, so Paul had much to say.

It became dark, so the people lit lamps. There were so many people in the building that Eutychus had to sit in an upstairs window.

Paul talked on and on. Eutychus nodded and

went to sleep—a sound sleep. He fell from the church window. Down, down, down, he went. It was a long fall. When the people picked him up, he was dead.

Paul rushed to Eutychus. He fell on him and put his arms around him. "Don't be worried," he said. "He's alive!"

Then Paul went upstairs and started talking again. He talked until the next day. When Paul left, the people took Eutychus home. They were glad for God's miracle.

Dear God, I thank You for my
church where I can learn about
You. Help me to listen to the
preacher as he reads from
the Bible. Amen.

A Snake Bites Paul

Paul gathered a pile of sticks and
was putting them on the fire when a
poisonous snake came out because of
the heat and bit him on the hand.

ACTS 28:3 NCV

What would you do if a snake bit you?
Would you be afraid? Paul wasn't afraid when a
snake bit him.

Paul was traveling on a ship when suddenly
a wild winter storm came up. *Whoo-oo, whoo-oo!*
The wind blew. The waves rose high. *Pitter-patter!*
Pitter-patter! The rain came down. The ship was
tossed around the sea.

Before the ship could reach land, it hit rocks
and broke into pieces. All the men on the ship
made it safely to the island.

The people on the island were kind. It was

cold and rainy, so they built a fire to keep the Paul and his shipmates warm. Paul picked up some sticks to throw on the fire. But a poisonous snake came out of the sticks and bit Paul's hand. Paul just brushed the snake off into the fire.

The people thought Paul was a bad man. They thought he would die from the snakebite. They watched him closely, but nothing happened to him. So Paul told the people he trusted in Jesus. A miracle had kept Paul safe from harm!

Dear God, I thank You for
miracles. I thank You for
keeping me safe from the bad
things in this world. Help me to
trust in You always. Amen.

Jane Landreth enjoys touching young lives with God's love. She taught school until her son was born, then officially launched a writing career using her son's adventures for story and article ideas. Later, other ideas came from teaching children in church. Jane and her husband, Jack, reside in the Ozarks, where she continues writing for children and teaches writing for a distance-learning school. This is her second book for Barbour Publishing—*Bible Prayers for Bedtime* was her first.

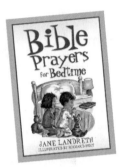